Managing Editor
Ina Massler Levin, M.A.

Editor-in-Chief
Sharon Coan, M.S. Ed.

Contributing Editor
Mara Ellen Guckian

Cover Artist
Barb Lorseyedi

Art Coordinator
Kevin Barnes

Illustrator
Renee Christine Yates

Imaging
Ralph Olmedo, Jr.

Product Manager
Phil Garcia

Publisher
Mary D. Smith, M.S. Ed.

Author

Lara L. Squires

Teacher Created Resources, Inc.
6421 Industry Way
Westminster, CA 92683
www.teachercreated.com
ISBN-13: 978-0-7439-3336-0
ISBN-10: 0-7439-3336-2
©2002 Teacher Created Resources, Inc.
Reprinted, 2006
Made in U.S.A.

Table of Contents

Introduction

A good understanding of phonics is the foundation of a successful reading career for your child. The more practice and exposure your child has with phonics concepts being taught in school, the more success he or she is likely to find. For many parents, knowing how to help their child can be frustrating because they don't have the resources or knowledge of how best to help. This series has been written with the parent in mind. It has been designed to help parents reinforce basic skills with their children. Students should have an understanding of single consonant sounds prior to beginning the exercises in this book. Basic phonics skills involving long vowels will be reviewed for kindergarteners and first graders. The exercises in this book can be done sequentially or can be taken out of order, as needed.

The following standards or objectives will be met or reinforced by completing the practice pages included in this book. These standards and objectives are similar to the ones required by your state and school district. These standards and objectives are appropriate for kindergarteners and first graders.

- Match long-vowel sounds to appropriate letters.
- Read simple one-syllable words.
- Distinguish long-vowel sounds in single-syllable words.
- Create and state rhyming words with long-vowel sounds.
- Add, delete, or change target sounds in order to change words.

How To Make the Most of This Book

Here are some useful ideas for making the most of this book:

- Set aside a specific place in your home to work on this book. Keep it neat and tidy with materials ready.
- Set up a certain time of day to work on these practice pages to establish consistency, or look for times in your day or week that are less hectic and more conducive to practicing skills.
- Keep all practice sessions with your child positive and constructive. If the mood becomes frustrated or tense, set the book aside and look for another time to practice with your child.
- Help beginning readers with instructions.
- Review the work your child has done and go over the answers together.
- Allow your child to use whatever writing instruments he or she prefers. For example, colored pencils can add variety and pleasure to drill work.
- Pay attention to the areas in which your child has the most difficulty. Provide extra guidance and exercises in those areas.
- Look for ways to make real-life application to the skills being reinforced. Play games with your child finding the vowel sounds in words. "Can you think of a dessert that begins with a *c* and has a long *a* sound?" CAKE!

Introducing Long ā

A long vowel says its name. Sometimes when a one-part word or syllable has two vowels, the first one is usually long and the second one is silent. The sound the *a* makes in *snail* is the long *a* sound. Sometimes, the consonant *y* pretends to be a vowel and makes the *a* in words like *play* say its name.

Review the long *a* pictures below (whale, quail, ape, snail, cake, snake). Color the pictures.

4

Identifying Long ā

Color the picture of each object that has a long *a* in its name.

Long ā World Scramble

Unscramble the letters to make long *a* words that are spelled with *ai*. Write the words on the line.

1. bdrai _____

2. nchia _____

3. laij _____

4. mila _____

5. anil _____

6. liap _____

7. ntpai _____

8. rani _____

9. lais _____

10. nsali _____

11. tila _____

12. tarni _____

Word Box

snail	chain	braid	sail	rain	tail
nail	jail	pail	mail	train	paint

Making "ay" Words

The letters *ay* can make the long *a* sound, as in the word *play*. Add *ay* to the letters below to make long *a* words. Write the word on the line.

1. b _____

2. d _____

3. h _____

4. l _____

5. m _____

6. p _____

7. pr _____

8. pl _____

9. r _____

10. s _____

11. st _____

12. tr _____

13. w _____

14. str _____

Rhyming Long ā Words

Find the words that rhyme with *snake*. Circle them.

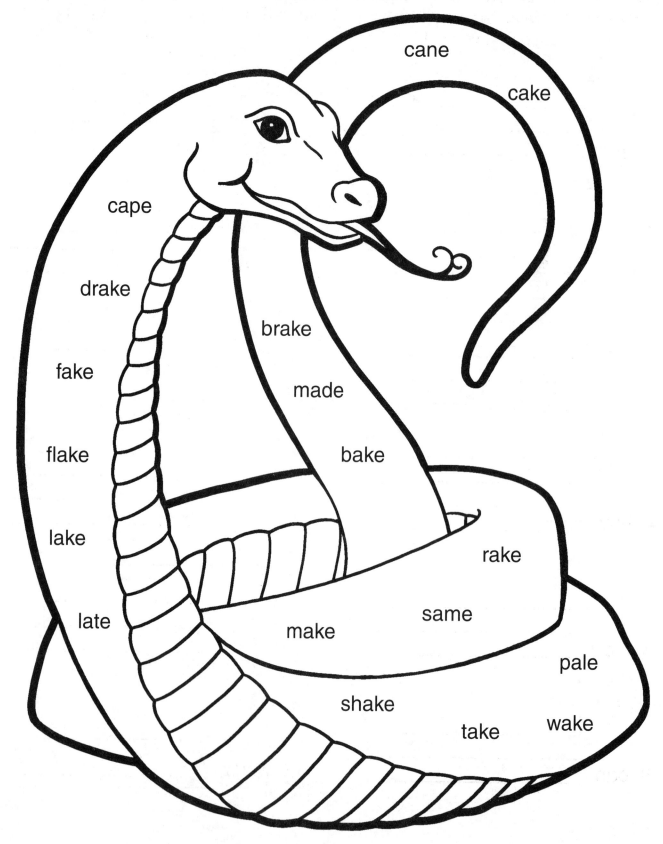

cane

cake

cape

drake

brake

fake

made

flake

bake

lake

rake

same

late

make

pale

shake

take

wake

8

Short ă and Long ā Words

An *e* can change a short vowel word into a long vowel word. Add a silent *e* to the end of each short *a* word. Write the long *a* words on the lines. Say the short vowel word and then the long vowel word. Listen for the difference.

1. can _____

2. cap _____

3. fad _____

4. mad _____

5. man _____

6. pan _____

7. past _____

8. plan _____

9. rat _____

10. tap _____

11. van _____

12. wag _____

Long ā Homonyms

A *homonym* is a word that sounds the same, but is spelled differently and means something different from another word. Write a silent *e* word that sounds the same as each of these words. Write the new word on the line.

1. gait _____

2. maid _____

3. mail _____

4. main _____

5. pail _____

6. pain _____

7. plain _____

8. sail _____

9. tail _____

10. waist _____

Introducing Long ē

A long vowel says its name. Sometimes when a one-part word or syllable has two vowels, the first one is usually long and the second one is silent. The sound the *e* makes in *seal* is the long *e* sound.

Review the long *e* pictures below (leaf, sea horse, seal, eel, zebra, eagle, sheep, peacock). Color the pictures.

Identifying Long ē

Color the picture of each object that has a long *e* in its name.

12

Making Long ē Words

The letters *ea* can make the long *e* sound. Fill in the missing letters to spell nine long *e* words.

1. ___ ea ___ ___

2. ea ___ ___ ___

3. ___ ea ___

4. ___ ea ___

5. ___ ea

6. ___ ea ___

7. ___ ea

8. ___ ea pod

9. ___ ea ___ ___

Long ē Word Search

The letters "ee" can make the long *e* sound. Unscramble the letters to spell long *e* words. Write the words on the lines.

1. ebet _____

2. dpee _____

3. teerg _____

4. jepe _____

5. pkee _____

6. mtee _____

7. deen _____

8. rede _____

9. rfee _____

10. sephe _____

11. thees _____

12. speel _____

13. dsee _____

14. rete _____

15. dewe _____

16. wepe _____

Word Box

weep	seed	sheet	deer	sleep	keep	greet	weed
tree	beet	reef	need	meet	jeep	deep	sheep

Long ē Crossword Puzzle Words

Fill in the crossword boxes with the correct letters.

1.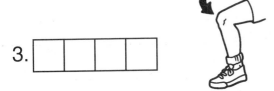

2.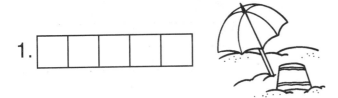

3.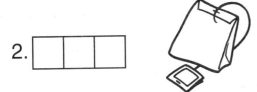

4.

5.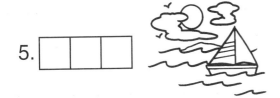

6.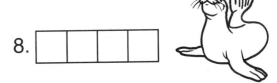

7.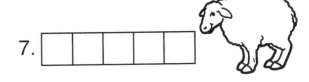

8.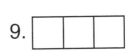

9.

10.

Word Box

knee	tree	pea	sheep	leaf
sleep	beach	seal	tea	sea

Introducing Long ī

A long vowel says its name. Sometimes when a one-part word or syllable has two vowels, the first one is usually long and the second one is silent. The sound the *i* makes in *spider* is the long *i* sound.

Review the long *i* pictures below (lion, rhino, spider, iron). Color the pictures.

Identifying Long ī

Color the picture of each object that has a long *i* in its name.

Completing the Sentence

Read the sentences. Write the missing words on the lines.

1. The ___ ___ ___ ___ can roar.

2. James has a ___ ___ ___ ___ .

3. I have ___ ___ ___ ___ toes.

4. Do you like to eat ___ ___ ___ ?

5. My dad wore a ___ ___ ___ .

6. The ___ ___ ___ ___ ate the cheese.

7. The ___ ___ ___ ___ grew on the gate.

8. Let's go fly a ___ ___ ___ ___ .

Word Box

bike	kite	pie	lion
five	mice	tie	vine

Rhyming Long ī Words

Write a rhyming word on each cherry. You may pick a word from the pie.

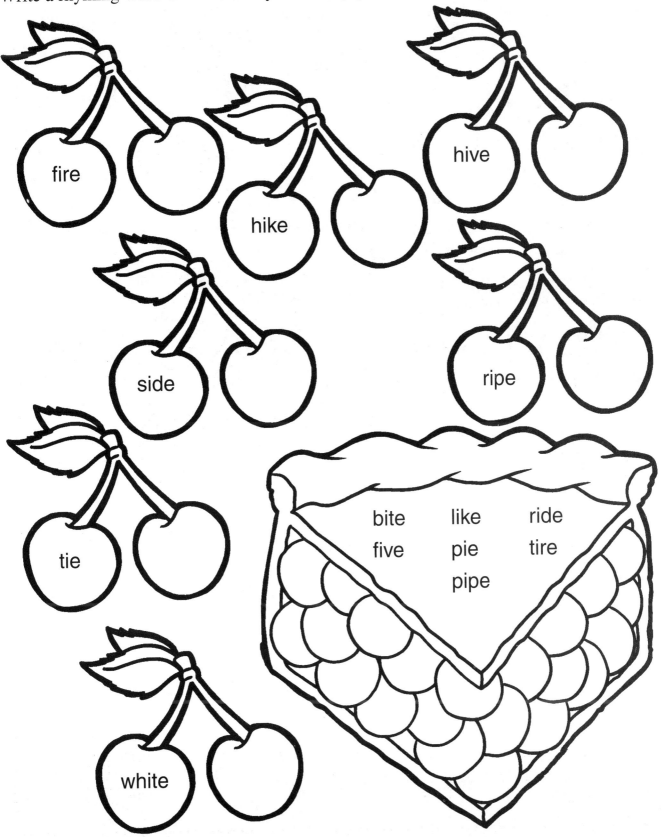

fire

hike

hive

side

ripe

tie

white

bite	like	ride
five	pie	tire
	pipe	

Making Long ī Words

An *e* is missing from each apple. Add a silent *e* to the end of each short *i* word to make words with the long *i* sound. Write the new long *i* words on the lines under the apples.

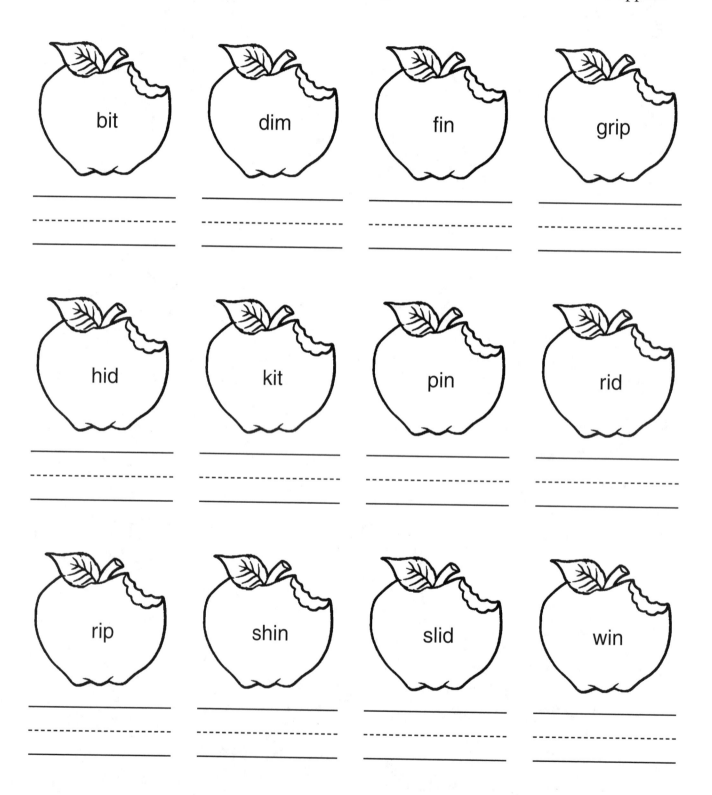

bit

dim

fin

grip

hid

kit

pin

rid

rip

shin

slid

win

20

Making "ie" Words

The letters *i* and *e* together can make the long *i* sound. Find these *ie* words in the puzzle. Circle the words as you find them. Read them out loud and listen to the long *i* sound.

cried	pie
die	skies
fried	tie
lie	tried

c	r	i	e	d	b	k	f
k	n	p	s	l	p	t	s
f	b	l	t	p	s	n	k
r	t	r	i	e	d	b	i
i	c	t	e	h	l	c	e
e	d	g	s	t	p	b	s
d	p	l	i	e	f	i	f
n	d	r	g	n	d	i	e

Introducing Long ō

A long vowel says its name. Sometimes when a one-part word or syllable has two vowels, the first one is usually long and the second one is silent. The sound the *o* makes in *goat* is the long *o* sound.

Review the long *o* words below (globe, cone, flamingo, goat, toad, boa). Color the pictures.

22

Identifying Long ō

Color the picture of each object that has a long *o* in its name.

Rhyming Long ō Words

Draw a line from the picture of a word in the first column to the word that rhymes with it in the second column.

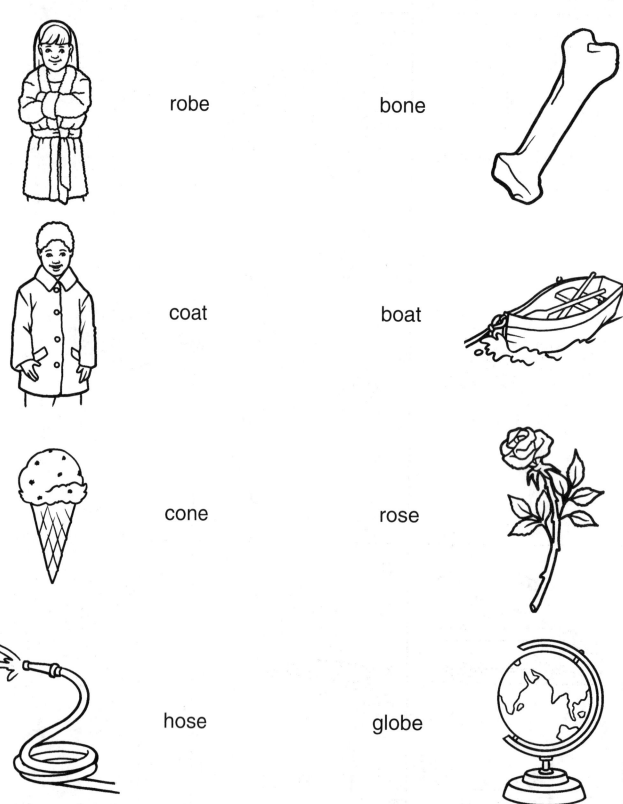

robe   bone

coat   boat

cone   rose

hose   globe

Making "oa" Words

The letters *oa* can make the long *o* sound. Fill in the missing letters to spell nine long *o* words.

1. ___ oa ___	2. ___ oa ___	3. ___ oa ___
4. ___ oa ___	5. ___ oa ___	6. ___ oa ___
7. ___ oa ___	8. ___ oa ___	9. ___ oa ___

Completing Long ō Words

Fill in the missing letters. Learn to spell all twelve long *o* words.

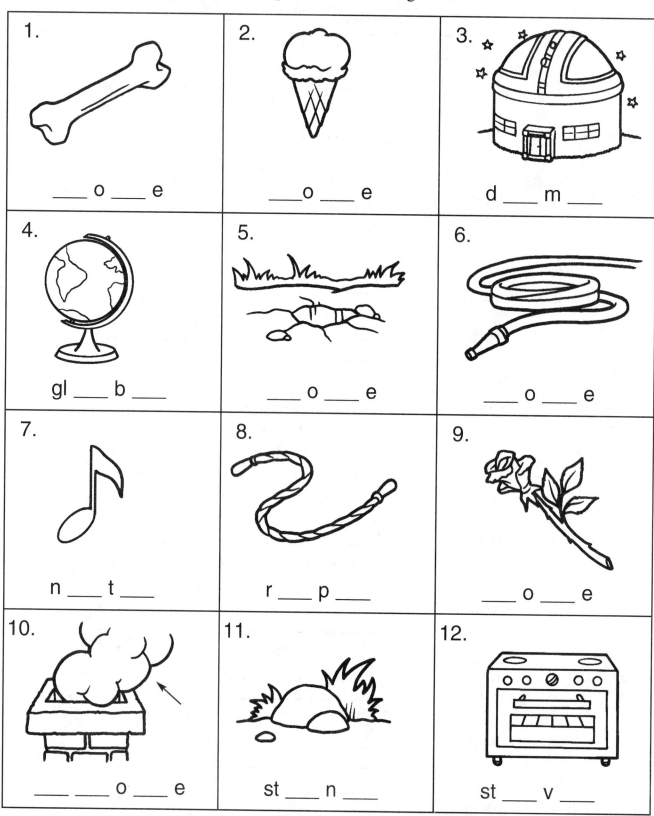

1. ___ o ___ e

2. ___ o ___ e

3. d ___ m ___

4. gl ___ b ___

5. ___ o ___ e

6. ___ o ___ e

7. n ___ t ___

8. r ___ p ___

9. ___ o ___ e

10. ___ ___ o ___ e

11. st ___ n ___

12. st ___ v ___

26

Long ō or Short ŏ?

Circle the long *o* word and write it on the line.

1. coat   cot

2. goat   got

3. rob   robe

4. hope   hop

5. ton   tone

6. globe   glob

7. not   note

8. rod   road

9. cod   code

10. cop   cope

11. mope   mop

12. con   cone

Introducing Long ū

A long vowel says its name. Sometimes when a one-part word or syllable has two vowels, the first one is usually long and the second one is silent. The sound the *u* makes in *mule* is the long *u* sound.

Review the long *u* pictures below (mule, music, June, unicorn, cube, juice). Color the pictures.

28

Identifying Long ū

Color the picture of each object that has a long *u* in its name.

Long ū Word Scramble

Unscramble these words to spell words with the long *u* sound. Write the words on the lines. Learn to spell these long *u* words.

1. cueb _____

2. tfuel _____

3. truif _____

4. uegl _____

5. uhge _____

6. Jneu _____

7. eulm _____

8. rdeu _____

9. elur _____

10. stiu _____

11. tbue _____

12. esu _____

Word Box

cube	flute	fruit	glue	huge	mule
use	tube	suit	rule	rude	June

Find the Real Long ū Word

Circle the real word. Write it on the line.

1. fune   tune   _____

2. cute   sube   _____

3. fuse   cuve   _____

4. hule   rule   _____

5. ruke   fruit   _____

6. sute   suit   _____

Long ū Puzzle

Use the words and picture clues given to complete the puzzle.

Across

2. 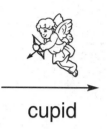 cupid

3. 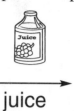 juice

5.  museum

8. cube

9.  tulip

Down

1. glue

2. cucumber

4. pupil

6. tutu

7. pupa

Long ū or Short ŭ?

Put an *X* over the words that have the short *u* sound. Color the boxes with long *u* words.

1. | blue | bug | cube | cut |

2. | cute | duck | flute | glue |

3. | huge | juice | June | sun |

4. | rub | rule | Sue | mule |

Introducing Y as a Vowel

When the letter *y* is the only vowel at the end of a one-syllable word such as *fly*, the *y* has the sound of a long *i*. When *y* is the only vowel at the end of a word of more than one syllable, such as *pony*, the *y* usually has a sound almost like long *e*. The names of the animals shown end in one of these two sounds.

Color the animal that ends with the long *i* sound black.

Color the animals that end with the long *e* sound brown.

Making Y = Long ī Words

Add *y* to the letters to spell words that end with the long *i* sounds. Learn how to spell all twelve words. Write each word two times.

1. b ___

2. cr ___

3. dr ___

4. fl ___

5. fr ___

6. m ___

7. sh ___

8. sk ___

9. sl ___

10. sp ___

11. tr ___

12. wh ___

Y = Long ē Words

If the *y* at the end of the word sounds like a long *e*, color the puppy brown. Color the other puppies gray.

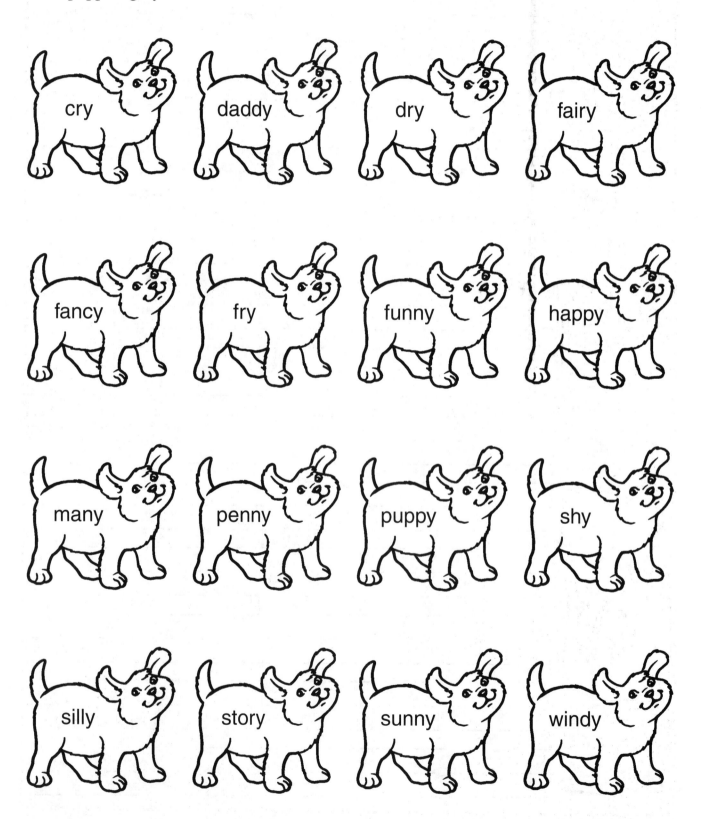

cry   daddy   dry   fairy

fancy   fry   funny   happy

many   penny   puppy   shy

silly   story   sunny   windy

Long Vowel Farm

How many long vowel words can you find in the picture?

Find the Missing Word

Read the sentence. Write the missing word on the line.

1. I have a __ __ __ __ __ on my face.

2. I use my __ __ __ __ at the beach.

3. I ate the __ __ __ __ .

4. Close the __ __ __ __ .

5. My __ __ __ __ is green.

6. I like to __ __ __ ice cream.

7. The __ __ __ __ grows into a tree.

8. The __ __ __ is in the hive.

9. The __ __ __ __ eat the cheese.

10. The __ __ __ __ has many leaves.

Word Box

bee	cake	gate	pail	smile
bike	eat	mice	seed	vine

Find the Missing Word

Read the sentence. Write the missing word on the line.

1. I like to play __ __ __ __ __.

2. I have __ __ __ __ toes on my foot.

3. The __ __ __ __ is in the hay.

4. The __ __ __ __ sails on the sea.

5. He __ __ __ __ up at five o'clock.

6. It will rain. Please put on your __ __ __ __ .

7. The __ __ __ __ carried bags on his back.

8. The child played with the __ __ __ __ in the water.

9. I play the __ __ __ __ __ .

10. The man wore a __ __ __ __ .

Word Box

five	boat	coat	flute	games
suit	woke	tube	mule	goat

Long ā and Long ē

Write the words in the correct columns.

Long ā	Long ē
_____	_____
_____	_____
_____	_____
_____	_____
_____	_____
_____	_____
_____	_____
_____	_____
_____	_____
_____	_____
_____	_____
_____	_____

Word Box

bag	bell	fair	please	jet	play	seed	ten	tree
beach	cane	gate	hay	leaf	sea	shape	tray	vase

40

Long Vowels ī, ō, and ū

Write the words in the correct columns.

Long ī	Long ō	Long ū

Word Box

bike	boat	bone	bug	coal
coat	cone	cute	drop	fire
five	flute	fly	fun	hop
huge	iron	lion	pig	plug
rule	ship	six	stone	stop
stove	suit	tire	true	tube

Test Practice 1

1.

Which long vowel sound do you hear in the picture word?

◯   ◯   ◯   ◯   ◯
a   e   i   o   u

2.

Which long vowel sound do you hear in the picture word?

◯   ◯   ◯   ◯   ◯
a   e   i   o   u

3.

Which long vowel sound do you hear in the picture word?

◯   ◯   ◯   ◯   ◯
a   e   i   o   u

4.

Which long vowel sound do you hear in the picture word?

◯   ◯   ◯   ◯   ◯
a   e   i   o   u

5.

Which long vowel sound do you hear in the picture word?

◯   ◯   ◯   ◯   ◯
a   e   i   o   u

Test Practice 2

1. Which long vowel sound do you hear in this picture word?

   ○ a   ○ e   ○ i   ○ o   ○ u

2. Which long vowel sound do you hear in this picture word?

   ○ a   ○ e   ○ i   ○ o   ○ u

3. Which long vowel sound do you hear in this picture word?

   ○ a   ○ e   ○ i   ○ o   ○ u

4. Which long vowel sound do you hear in this picture word?

   ○ a   ○ e   ○ i   ○ o   ○ u

5. Which long vowel sound do you hear in this picture word?

   ○ a   ○ e   ○ i   ○ o   ○ u

Test Practice 3

Read the words from Word List 1 to an adult. (Cover Word List 2) Place a check mark (✓) by the words read correctly. Practice the unchecked words on the lines below. Repeat the process with Word List 2.

Word List 1		Word List 2	
1. bee	_____	1. pole	_____
2. mule	_____	2. game	_____
3. rose	_____	3. lake	_____
4. fire	_____	4. see	_____
5. pail	_____	5. rope	_____
6. kite	_____	6. tire	_____
7. cape	_____	7. cute	_____
8. rake	_____	8. bead	_____

Word Practice

_____
_____

_____
_____

_____
_____

_____
_____

_____
_____